The Paddy Reilly Songbook

Exclusive Distributors:

Music Sales Limited
8/9 Frith Street, London, W1V 5TZ, England

Music Sales Corporation,
225 Park Avenue South, 18th Floor, New York, NY10003, USA

Music Sales Pty Limited
120 Rothschild Street, Roseberry, NSW 2018, Australia.

CONWAY EDITIONS
New York/London/Sydney

Contents

Music Setting .... Seton Music Graphics
Design .... Niche Ltd.
Produced by Pat Conway.

The Flight Of Earls

Words & Music
Liam Reilly

Moderato

I can hear the bells of Dub- lin_____ In this lone- ly wait _ ing room, And the pa- per boys_____ are sing- ing in the rain _____ Not too long be- fore they take us_____ to the air - port and __ the noise, _____ to

This arrangement © 1989 Conway Editions

3

get on board a trans - at-lan - tic plane _____

(1) We've got
(2) So the
(3) But the

no - thing left to stay for, _____ we have no more _____ left to say, And there

is - n't an - y work for us to do _____ So fare

well ye boys and girls _____ An- oth- er blood- y flight _ of earls. Our best

as- set   is   our   best ____ ex- port   too _____

It's not murder, fear or famine
That makes us leave this time
We're not going to join MacAlpine's Fusiliers
We've got brains and we've got vision
We've got education too
But we just can't throw away these precious years.

So we walk the streets of London
And the streets of Baltimore
And we meet at night in several Boston bars
We're the leaders of the future
But we're far away from home
And we dream of you beneath the Irish stars.

As we look on Ellis Island
And the lady in the bay
And Manhattan turns to face another Sunday
We just wonder what you're doing
For to bring us all back home.
As we look forward to another Monday.

But it's not the work that scares us
We don't mind an honest job
And we know things will get better once again
So a thousand times adieu
We've got Bono and U2
All we're missing is the Guiness and the rain.

So switch off your new computers
'Cause the writing's on the wall
We're leaving as our fathers did before
Take a look at Dublin airport
Or the boat that leaves North Wall
There'll be no youth unemployment any more

Because we're over here in Queensland
And in parts of New South Wales
We're on the seas, the airways and the trains
But if we see better days
Those big airplanes go both ways
And we'll all be coming back to you again.
Yes we'll all be coming back to you again.

Cavan Girl

Words & Music
Tom Moore

As I walked the road from Kil - le-shan-ra wea-ry I sit down For it's twelve long miles a-round the lake to get to Ca-van town. The wa-ter and ___ the road I go once seen be-yond com-pare now I

curse the time it takes to reach my Ca- van girl so fair.

As I walk the road from Kilashandra, weary I sit down
For it's twelve long miles around the lake, to get to Cavan town
Through Oughter and the road I go, once seen beyond compare
Now I curse the time it takes to reach, my Cavan girl so fair.

The autumn shades are on the leaves, the trees will soon be bare
And each red coat leaf around me seems, the colour of her hair
My gaze retreats defies my feet and once again I sigh
Of a broken pool of sky reminds; The colour of her eyes.

At the Cavan cross each Sunday morning, it's there sha can be found
And she seems to have the eye of every boy in Cavan town
If my luck will hold I'll have the golden summer of her smile
And to break the hearts of Cavan men she'll talk to me a while.

So next Sunday evening finds me homeward Kilashandra bound
To work a week 'till I return to court in Cavan town
When asked if she would be my bride at least she'd not said no
So next Sunday morning 'rouse myself and back to her I go.

The Rose of Allendale

Trad.
arr. Paddy Reilly

left _____ her High land home and wan-dered forth ___ with

me _____ Oh the flow - ers decked the moun - tain -

side and fra-grance filled _____ the vale _____ By___

far _____ the sweet - est Flo - wer there was the rose___ of

Al- _____ len dale _____ Sweet Rose of Al - len -

dale _____ Sweet Rose _____ of Al- _____ len - dale _____

_____ By_____ far _____ the sweet - est flo-_____ wer

there _____ was the Rose _____ of Al-_____ len - dale _____

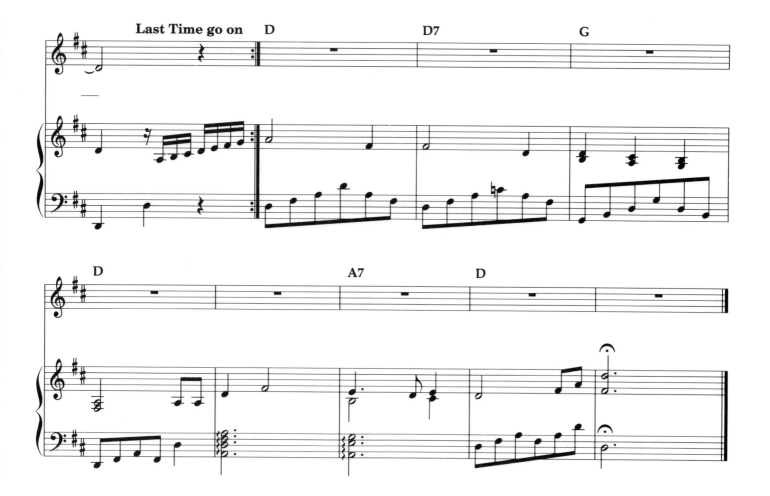

Where'er I wandered, to the east or the west, and fate began to lower,
Consoling still she was to me in sorrow's lonely hour.
Oh tempests wrecked my lonely boat and wrecked the quivering sail
One maiden form withstood the storm, 'twas the Rose of Allendale.

Chorus

And when my fever'd lips were parched on Africa's burning sands,
She whispered hopes of happiness and tales of foreig ànds
My life had been a wilderness, unblest by fortune's gain,
Had fate not linked my knot to hers, sweet Rose of Allendale.

Chorus

Beautiful Dreamer

Words & Music by
Stephen Foster

The Green Island

Words & Music by
Jimmy Crowley

Verse

No - bod - y knows the ans- wers _____ of the dark clouds keep rol - ling each day _____ Cas - ting a sha-dow___ u - po-n us _____ From

An- trim to sweet Ban - try Bay _____ In their

droves all the peo - ple are le - a- ving _____ Sure 'tis

worse than the black for - ty four _____ When they

sailed a - way o - ver ___ the o - cea - n _____. With their

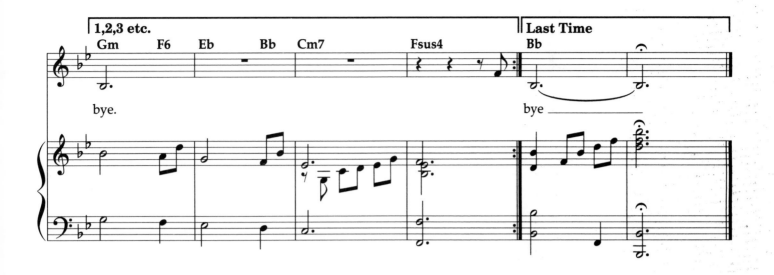

Nobody knows the answers
Of the dark clouds keep rolling each day
Casting a shadow upon us
From Antrim to sweet Bantry Bay
In their droves all the people are leaving
Sure 'tis worse than the black forty-four
When they sailed away over the ocean
With their dreams and their humble sea stories.

Chorus

What a legacy, such a tragedy
Thousands are saying goodbye
The land of the eagle is calling
As we bid the Green Island goodbye.

It's only six hours to Boston
And if you serve your time on the plane
In no time at all your a chippy
As good as the rest at the game.
It's Sally O'Briens we'll be dancing
But we'll go back some day maybe when
The blue moon it hangs over Dublin
And the river runs up Spancill Hill

Repeat Chorus

Is this a good time to remember
The great men and women who died.
Whose vision is misrepresented.
By the shadows who flicker and hide
They dish out their perks and their pensions
While the big fella turns in his grave
To see the bright diamonds and jewels
Cast on the cold crest of a wave.

My Lovely Rose of Clare

Trad.
arr. Paddy Reilly

Oh my love - ly Rose of Clare_____ you're the sweet - est girl I know You're the Queen of all the ro-__ ses like the pret - ty flowers that grow you are the sun- shine

Oh the sun it shines out like a jewel, on the lovely hills of Clare.
As I strolled along with my sweet lass, one evening at the fair
Her eyes they shone like silver streams, her long and golden hair
For I have won the heart of one, my lovely Rose of Clare.

Chorus

As we walked down by the river bank, watched the Shannon flowing by,
And listened to the nightingale, singing songs for you and I
And to say farewell to all you true and fair,
For I have stolen the heart of one, my lovely Rose of Clare.

The Old Refrain

Words & Music by
Brandle/Kerisler

1st Time Repeat
Last Time Go On

sat _____ a - lone a - long my way _____ as long as

I can sing _____ the old E A

23

I often think about the ode
When I am all alone and far away
I sing an old refrain the ode
And it recalls to me of bygone days
It takes me back again to meadows fair
Where sunlight's golden rays beam everywhere
My childhood joys again come back to me
My mother's face in fancy too I see

It was my mother taughter me how to sing
And to that memory my heart will cling
I never sat alone while on my way
As long as I can sing the ode.

Though years have passed and gone the ode
Although my heart is young my hair is grey
And still the echoes ring the ode
And dearful memories forever stay
My song can bring me visions full of light
And sweetest dreams throughout the darkest night
Although but life can give of summer's best
I'll take it with me when I go to rest.

And when at last my journey here is o'er
Will ring more joyfully that ere before
And up to heaven I will make my way
The angels too will sing the ode.

The Flower of Sweet Strabane

Trad.
arr. Paddy Reilly

If I were king _____ of Ire- land and all _____ things at my will. I'd

roam through all cre - a- tion new

com - forts to _____ find still _____ and the

com - fort I would seek _____ the most _____ as

you might un- _____ der - stand _____ is to

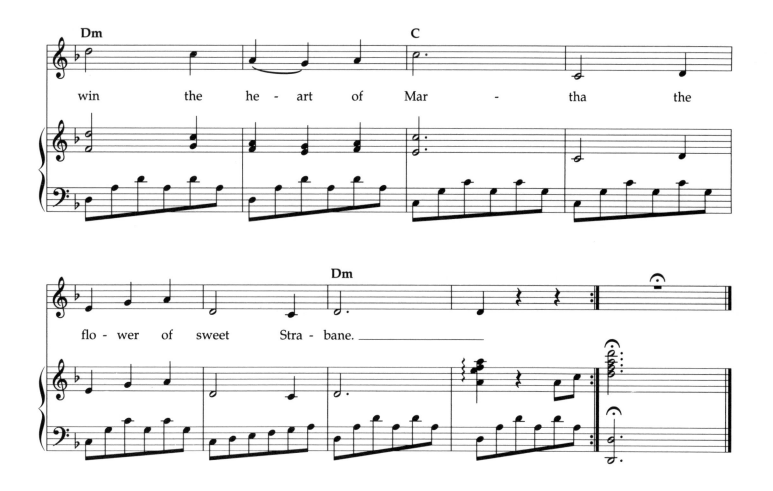

win   the   he - art   of   Mar   -   tha   the

flo - wer   of   sweet   Stra - bane.

Her cheeks they are a rosy red, her hair a lovely brown
And oe'r her milk white shoulders it carelessly hangs down
She's one of the fairest creatures in the whole of Ireland
And my heart is captivated by the Flower of Sweet Strabane.

If I had you lovely Martha away in Innisowen
Or in some lonesome valley in the wild woods of Tyrone
I would use my whole endeavour to try to work my plan
For to gain my prize and feast my eyes on the Flower of sweet Strabane.

But I'll go o'er the Lagan down by the steam ships tall
I'm sailing for Amerikay what ever may befall
My boat is bound for Liverpool right by the Isle of Man
So I'll say farewell, God bless you, my Flower of sweet Strabane.

The Old Rustic Bridge

Trad.
arr. Paddy Reilly

Flowing

I'm think - ing to - night of the old rus- tic bridge that bends o'er the mur - mur - ing stream _____ 'Twas there Mag- gie dear with our hearts full of cheer we

strayed 'neath the moon's gen - tle gleam _____ 'twas

there I first met you, ___ the light in your eyes a -

woke in my heart a sweet trill _____ Though

now far a - way still my thoughts fond - ly stray to the

29

old rus- tic bridge by the mill _____ Be -

neath it the stream gen - tly riples _____ a -

round it the birds love to trill _____ Though

getting slower

original speed

now far a - way still my thoughts fond - ly

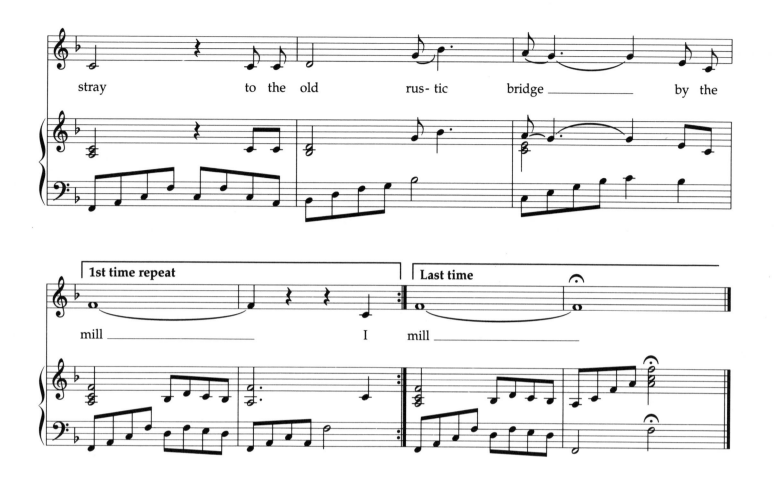

stray   to the old   rus- tic   bridge _____ by the

1st time repeat   **Last time**

mill _____   I   mill _____

I keep it in me memory, our love of the past
With me it's as bright as of old.
For deep in my heart, it was planted to last
In absence it never grows cold.
I think of you darling, while lonely at night
When all is peaceful and still.
My heart wanders back, in a dream of delight
To the old rustic bridge by the mill.

Beneath it the stream gently ripples etc.

The Fields of Athenry

Words & Music
Pete St. John

By a lonely prison wall
I heard a young man calling
Mary nothing matters when you're free
Against the famine and the crown
I rebelled they ran me down

Chorus

By a lonely harbour wall
She watched the last star falling
As the prison ship sailed out against the sky
Sure she'll live and hope and pray
For her love in Botany Bay
It's so lonely round the fields of Athenry

Chorus

The Snowy-Breasted Pearl

Trad.
arr. Paddy Reilly

But a kiss with welcome bland
And touch of Thy fair hand
Are all that I demand would'st thou not scorn
But, if not mine dear girl
My snowy breasted pearl
May I never from the fair with life return.

If to France or far off Spain
She crossed the watery main
To see her face again the seas I'd brave.
But if not mine dear girl
Oh, snowy breasted pearl
May I never from the fair with life return.

Come Back Paddy Reilly

Words & Music
Percy French
arr. Paddy Reilly

turn to the left at____ the bridge of ____ Fin - ea and

stop when half way to Coote Hill _____ 'Tis

there you will find it, I know sure en - ough for

for- tune____ has come to my call _____ the

40

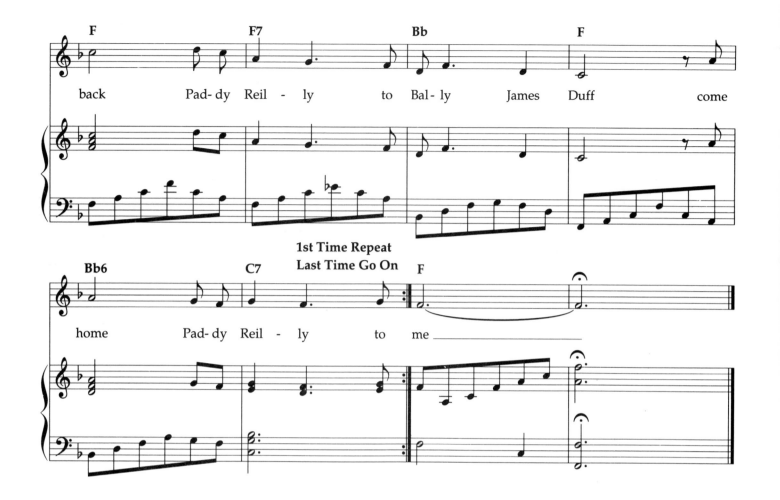

My mother once told me that when I was born
The day that I first saw the light
I looked down the street on that very first morn
And gave a great crow of delight
Now most new-born babies appear in a huff
And start with a sorrowful squall.
But I knew I was born in Ballyjamesduff
And that's why I smiled at them all!
The baby's a man now, he's toil worn and tough
Still whispers come over the sea.

Come back Paddy Reilly to Ballyjamesduff
Come home Paddy Reilly to me.

Matt Hyland

Trad.
arr. Paddy Reilly

cour - ted by _____ a _____ fair young man _____ who

was a ser - vant to her fa_____ ther_____ but when her

par - ents came to know_____ They swore they'd

ban him from the is-_____ land. The _____

So straight away to her love she goes, into his room to awake him
Saying "arise my love and go away, this very night you will be taken.
I overheard my parents say, in spite of me they will transport you
So arise my love and go away, I wish to God I'd gone before you."

They both sat down upon the bed, just for the side of one half hour
And not a word did either speak as down their cheeks their tears did shower
She laid her head upon his breast, around his neck her arms entwined
Not a duke nor lord nor an earl I'll wed, I'll wait for you my own Matt Hyland.

The Lord discoursed with his daughter fair, one night alone in her bed chamber
Saying "we'll give you leave for to bring him back, since there's no one can win your favour
She wrote a letter then in haste, for him her heart was still repining
They brought him back, to the church they went, and made a lord of young Matt Hyland.

The Little Grey Home In The West

Trad.
arr. Paddy Reilly

road may _____ be long,   in the lilt of   the song,   I for-
get   I was wear-y   be - fore _____ Far a-
head   where the blue sha - dows fail _____ I shall
come   to con- tent- ment   and rest.   And   the

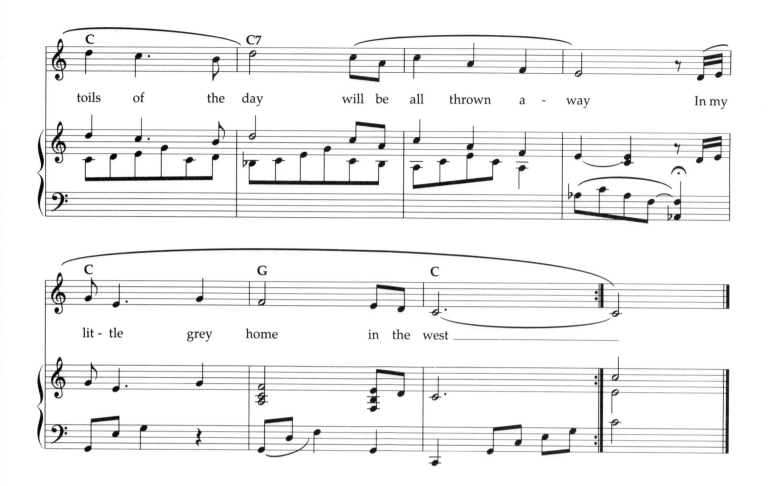

toils of the day will be all thrown a - way In my

lit - tle grey home in the west

There are arms that will welcome me in
There are lips that I'm burning to kiss
There are two eyes that shine
Just because they are mine
And a thousand things other than this
It's a corner of heaven itself
Though it's only a tumbled down nest
But with love blooming there
Why no place can compare
With my little grey home in the west.

O'Connell's Steam Engine

Trad.
arr. Paddy Reilly

Oh peo - ple of heart I pray pay at - ten - tion lis - ten to what I'm a - bout to re - late

gap she was mil - king her cow _____ she was

jig - ging that tune called "Make haste to the wed- ding" or

some oth - er dit- ty, I can't tell you now _____

Ah the next came along, it was a bold tinker
Who happen'd by chance to be passing that way
The day being fine they sat down together
What news of that man the old woman did say
There's no news at all mam replied the bold tinker
But the people all wish that he never had been
He a dam of a rogue is that Daniel
And he's now making babies in Dublin by steam.

Ah the children are ruined replied the ould woman
Or has the quare fellow gone crazy at last
Or is it the sign of a war or a rebellion
For what is the reason he want's them so fast
It's not that at all Mam replied the bould tinker
The children of Ireland are getting too small
It's O'Connells petition to the new Lor Lieutenant
That he won't let us make them the old way at all.

By this pipe in me mouth replied the ould woman
And that's a strong oath on me soul for to say
But I am an auld woman and I was near him
I bet you my life that he'd rue the day
For the people of Ireland they're very well known
They gave him their earnings when needing them bad
And now that he is recompensing them for it
By taking the only diversion they had.

Light to you coach Mam replied the Bould tinker
Long may you live now with youth on your side
If all the young girls in Ireland were like you
O'Connell could trow his steam engine aside
If I had the young men of Ireland around me
And girls making babies as fast as they can
And whenever Her Majesty wanted an army
We'd be able to send her as many as Dan.

The Lark In The Morning

Trad.
arr Paddy Reilly

The lark___ in the mor - ning she ris - es off her nest and she goes home___ in the eve - ning with the dew all on her breast___ And like the jol - ly plough - boy she whist - les and she sings and she goes

Oh Roger the ploughboy he is a dashing blade
He goes whistling and singing in yonder green lane
Oh he met pretty young Susan she's handsome I declare
She's far more enticing than the birds in the air.

Chorus
When twenty six weeks they were over and passed
Her mother asked the reason why she thickened round the waist
Oh it was the handsome ploughboy this young girl she did say
For he caused for to tumble all in the new mown hay

Chorus
Here's a health to young ploughboys wherever you may be
That likes to have a bonnie lass a sittin on his knee
With a glass of good strong porter you'll whistle and you'll sing
For a ploughboy is as happy as a prince or a king.

Sweet Carnlough Bay

Trad.
arr. Paddy Reilly

When win - ter was braw - ling oe'r high hills and moun - tains, _____ and dark were the clouds oe'r the deep roll - ing sea _____ I spied a wee

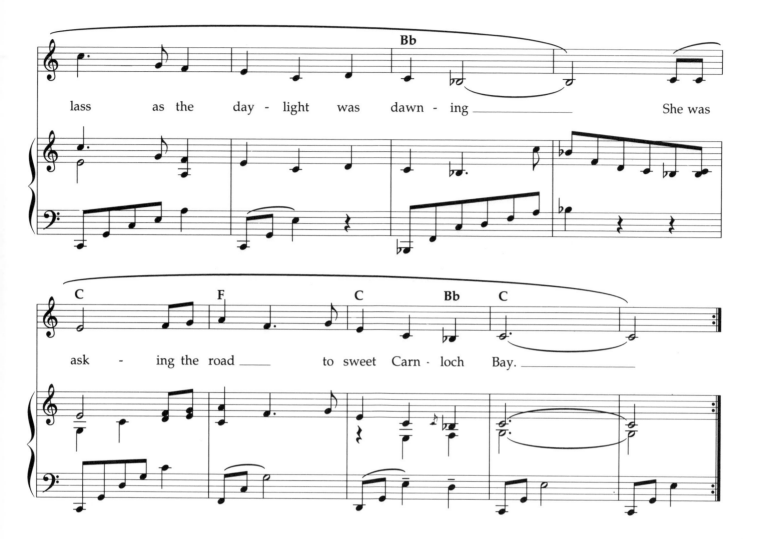

lass   as the   day - light   was   dawn - ing _____ She was

ask - ing the road _____ to sweet Carn - loch Bay. _____

I said, 'my fair lass, I surely will tell you
The road and the number of miles it will be
And if you'll consent I'll convey you a wee bit
And I'll show you the way to sweet Carnloch Bay.

You turn to the right and go down to the church yard
Cross over the river and down by the sea
We'll stop at Pat Hamill's and have a wee drop there
Just to help us along to sweet Carnloch Bay.

Here's a health to Pat Hamill, likewise the dear lassie
And all you young ladies who're listening to me
And ne'er turn your back on a bonnie young lassie
When she's asking the road to sweet Carnloch Bay.

The Longford Weaver

Trad.
arr. Paddy Reilly

These___ five long Quar - ters I have been wea - vin', and for my wea_____ vin' I was paid

down. I bought a shirt in the fore-most fash - ion all for to

walk___ up to Long-ford Town, I walked___ up and through Long-ford

Ci - ty where Nan - cy's whisk-___ ey I chanc'd to smell. I thought it

fun for to go and taste it, these five long quar-___ ters I liked it

I entered in to a little ale house
Begged Nancy's pardon for making free
And Nancy met me at every corner
Your hearty welcome young man said she
We both sat down at a little table
We looked at t'other a little while
We both sat down at a little table
And Nancy's whiskey did me beguile.

I found myself then in a little corner
I found myself then in a little bed
I tried to rise but I was not able
For Nancy's whiskey held down my head
When I arose aye the following morning
I asked the reckoning I had to pay
It's fifteen shillings for ale and porter
And pay it quickly now and get away.

I put my hand in to my pocket
The ready money I laid it down
it's fifteen shillings for ale and porter
And all remaining was a half-a-crown
Well I looked up and looked down the window
Where there a fair maid I chanced to spy
I called her in and spent two and two-pence
And all remaining was a crooked by.

I put the money upon the table
Saying I'll leave this money out with the rest
I'll drink a health to every young man
And every lassie that the best, the best
And I'll go home, I'll begin my weaving
I'll stil me shuttle another while
And if I live through another season
It's Nancy's whiskey will not me beguile.

Sam Hall

Trad.
arr. Paddy Reilly

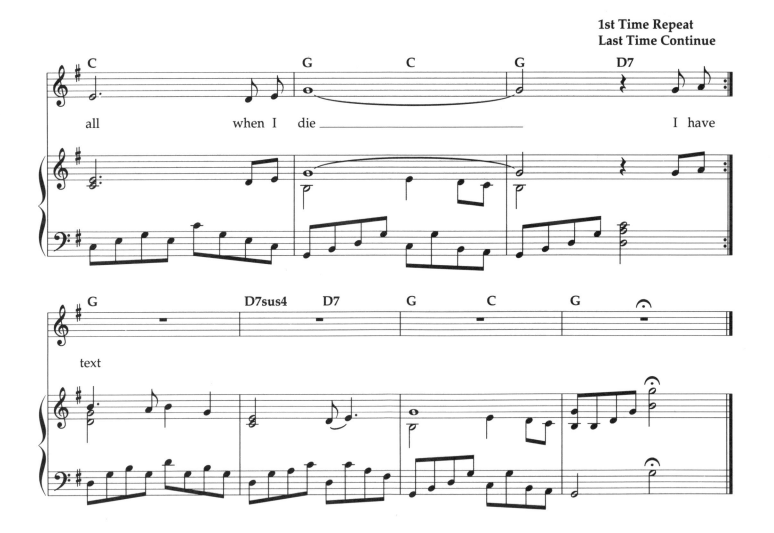

all   when I die _____   I have

text

I have twenty pounds in store, that's not all, that's not all
I have twenty pounds in store, that's not all
I have twenty pounds in store and I'll rob for twenty more
For the rich must help the poor, so must I, so must I,
For the rich must help the poor, so must I.

Up the ladder I did grope, that's no joke, that's no joke
Up the ladder I did grope, that's no joke
Up the ladder I did grope and the hangman pulled his rope
And ne'er a word I spke, tumbling down, tumbling down
And ne'er a word I spoke tumbling down.

Oh they brought me to Cootehill in a cart, in a cart.
Oh they brought me to Cootehill ina cart
Oh they brought me to Cootehill and I stopped to make my will
For the best of friends must part, so must I, so must I
For the best of friends must part, so must I

Repeat first verse

Pat Murphy's Meadow

Trad.
arr. Paddy Reilly

When the Aut - umn days are here a - gain and the night wind chil - ly blows, ___ The wood-lands turn to gol-___ den hue and the har - vests moon a - glow ___ To hear a - gain of days ___ long past to come no more I

know,   When I mowed   Pat Mur-phy's   mea-dow _____ In the sun-ny   long   a-

go _____   I   Where   Those

I see again the ocean
And the distant sails afar
As the maiden in the meadow
Strikes up
There was music soft and tender
In the winds that whispered low
When I mowed Pat Murphy's meadow
In the sunny long ago.

Where are the happy boys and girls
That danced the gay quadrills
Or the singer that warbled sweetly
In the burning granite mill
To hear again at sunset
Where sweet afton waters flow
When I mowed Pat Murphy's meadow
In the sunny long ago.

Those days are golden memories
Like the snows of yester years
And when evening shades are falling
All alone I shed a tear
On my cheek I feel the soft touch
Of the winds that whisper low
When I mowed Pat Murphy's meadow
In the sunny long ago.